# Twelve Angry Men

by
Reginald Rose

# Teacher Guide

Written by
Pat Watson

## Note

The 2006 Penguin Classic Books paperback edition of the drama, © 1955, 1997 by Reginald Rose, with Introduction by David Mamet, © 2006 by David Mamet, was used to prepare this guide. Page references may differ in other editions. ISBN 0-14-310440-3

**Please note:** This drama deals with sensitive, mature issues. Parts contain profanity and/or descriptions of violence. Please assess the appropriateness of this play for the age level and maturity of your students prior to reading and discussing it with them.

ISBN 978-1-60539-062-8

To order, contact your local school supply store, or—

Novel Units, Inc.
P.O. Box 97
Bulverde, TX 78163-0097

Web site: www.novelunits.com

# Table of Contents

# Skills and Strategies

## Thinking
Brainstorming, analysis, compare/contrast, research, critical thinking, evaluation, conflict

## Comprehension
Prediction, cause/effect, inference, plot development, thematic development, conflict/resolution

## Literary Elements
Metaphor, simile, symbolism, irony, characterization, tone, setting, theme, hyperbole, genre, sarcasm, rhetorical question

## Vocabulary
Target words, definitions, application

## Listening/Speaking
Discussion, report, script performance, reenactment, interview

## Writing
Poetry, script, monologue, letter, editorial, newspaper article, review

## Across the Curriculum
Music—appropriate background selections; Art—blueprint, collage, diorama, sketch

## Viewing
Movie version of *Twelve Angry Men*

**Genre:** drama

**Setting:** jury room of a New York court of law; very hot summer day in 1957

**Themes:** justice, prejudice, integrity, common sense, anger, democratic process

**Conflict:** person vs. person, person vs. society, person vs. self

**Tone:** realistic; changes from pessimistic to optimistic

**Date of First Publication:** 1955—as a one-hour drama for CBS's *Studio One*; 1957—first film version

## Summary

Twelve jurors must decide the fate of a 16-year-old boy who is on trial for allegedly killing his father. If convicted by a unanimous vote of the jurors, he will receive an automatic death sentence. Only one man, Juror #8, votes "not guilty" when the first vote is taken. Throughout the jury's proceedings, he attempts to cast "reasonable doubt" on the defendant's guilt. To do so, he must circumvent the apathy, prejudice, and bias of the other jurors. Although initially appearing to be an unlikely ally, Juror #9 supports Juror #8 as several jurors reveal ambiguities in the prosecution's case. One by one, the other jurors begin to have reasonable doubt about the defendant's guilt and change their votes to "not guilty." The jury reaches a unanimous verdict when the lone dissenter, Juror #3, finally agrees with the others.

## About the Playwright

**Personal:** Reginald Rose was born in New York City in 1920. He attended Townsend Harris High School and City College before enlisting in the U.S. Army after Pearl Harbor. He served in the Philippines and Japan, attaining the rank of First Lieutenant. He was married twice and had six children. He died in 2002 from complications of a heart condition.

**Career:** Rose, an American film and television writer, began writing when he was a teenager. He sold his first television play, *The Bus to Nowhere*, in 1950 and was most well-known for his work in the early years of television drama. He served on a jury for the first time in 1954—a manslaughter case. Jurors argued angrily for eight hours before reaching a unanimous verdict. Capturing the powerful situation in the jury room, Rose wrote *Twelve Angry Men* as a one-hour drama for CBS's *Studio One,* and the film version was made in 1957. Stage productions of *Twelve Angry Men* include the original in 1964 and revised versions in 1996 and 2004. Rose's work in television included writing a broad spectrum of dramas and the creation, supervision, and writing of many episodes of the TV series *The Defenders* from 1961–1965. He wrote the screenplay for several films, including *Crime in the Streets, The Wild Geese, The Sea Wolves, Man of the West, Somebody Killed Her Husband,* and *Whose Life Is It Anyway?* He also wrote *Six Television Plays* (1957) and *The Thomas Book* (1972). In addition to his stage production of *Twelve Angry Men,* Rose's writing for theater included *Black Monday* (1962), *The Porcelain Year* (1965), *Dear Friends* (1968), and *This Agony, This Triumph* (1972). He also wrote for children and published a memoir, *Undelivered Mail.*

**Honors:** Rose received Oscar nominations for Best Screenplay and Best Picture (as co-producer) for *Twelve Angry Men.* He was nominated for six Emmy awards and won three (1954, 1962, 1963). A sampling of his many honors includes the Berlin Film Festival Golden Bear, three Mystery Writers of America Awards (including the Edgar Allan Poe Award), Writers Guild of America Awards (including the Lifetime Achievement Award), and the Writers Guild of America Laurel Award in 1958 and 1987.

# Characters

(**Note:** Jurors are known by their numbers only.)

**Juror #1 (Foreman):** assistant head football coach; preoccupied with his jury responsibilities; tries to accommodate others and keep peace

**Juror #2:** nervous and timid; has never served on a jury; initially thinks defendant is guilty because "nobody proved otherwise"; disapproves of other jurors' jokes

**Juror #3:** owns a messenger service; volatile, opinionated, and obstinate; shows prejudice against "those kids" and is convinced the defendant is a dangerous killer; thinks the case is open-and-shut and wants to finish quickly; has one son from whom he is estranged

**Juror #4:** stockbroker; intelligent, self-assured, and rational; tries to calm others

**Juror #5:** nurse in a Harlem hospital; young man who has grown up in the slums

**Juror #6:** housepainter; makes up his mind immediately but is respectful toward others; thinks argument between defendant and victim is a strong motive

**Juror #7:** salesman; avid sports fan who is more interested in getting to a baseball game than justice for the defendant; impatient and cynical; vows his vote is unchangeable

**Juror #8:** architect; only juror to vote "not guilty" initially; logical and consistent; searches for the truth; remains calm under pressure

**Juror #9:** elderly; observant, sensible, and concerned; first to agree with Juror #8

**Juror #10:** owns three garages; sarcastic, impatient, and bigoted; paranoid about people from the slums; loud and volatile

**Juror #11:** watchmaker; immigrant from Europe who is proud to serve on the jury; sensitive to others; rational and sensible

**Juror #12:** works in advertising; impressed by prosecuting attorney; indecisive

# Background Information

The following information will enhance students' understanding of the play.

## Legal Terms

1. trial by jury (guaranteed by the 6th Amendment to the United States Constitution): "In all criminal prosecutions, the accused shall enjoy the right to a speedy and public trial, by an impartial jury of the State and district wherein the crime shall have been committed, which district shall have been previously ascertained by law, and to be informed of the nature and cause of the accusation; to be confronted with the witnesses against him; to have compulsory process for obtaining witnesses in his favor, and to have the Assistance of Counsel for his defense."

2. open-and-shut case: simple and direct; there is an obvious answer to all questions involved

3. public defender: attorney appointed by the court and paid from public funds to defend persons who cannot afford to hire their own attorneys

4. public prosecutor: attorney for the government; district attorney or his/her assistant who prosecutes the accused

5. burden of proof: obligation to provide evidence; In a criminal case, the prosecuting attorney has the burden of proving the defendant's guilt beyond a reasonable doubt.

6. eyewitness testimony: report given by someone who actually saw a crime being committed

7. circumstantial evidence: evidence that depends on circumstances surrounding a crime; Circumstantial evidence is inconclusive without the help of other evidence, e.g., the witness might have seen the defendant leaving the murder scene, indicating that he or she could have killed the victim, but this evidence alone will not prove the crime.

8. reasonable doubt: doubt based on reasoning or logic

9. hung jury: jury that cannot reach a unanimous decision and is dismissed

**Literary Terms**

1. elements of drama:

   (a) a story

   (b) told in action

   (c) played out by actors who impersonate the characters of the story

2. plot development:

   (a) exposition: creates tone, gives setting, introduces most characters, provides background information necessary to understand the play, e.g., events that have taken place before the play begins

   (b) rising action (complication): successive stages of conflict between the protagonist and other characters leading to the climax

   (c) climax: turning point

   (d) falling action: steps that lead logically to the resolution

   (e) denouement (resolution): explanation of outcome

3. protagonist: leading or main character

4. antagonist: the character who contends against the protagonist; adversary; There can be more than one antagonist.

5. types of irony:

   (a) verbal: contrast between what the character says and what s/he means

   (b) dramatic: contrast between what the character thinks is true and what the reader or viewer knows is true, i.e., the viewer knows more than the character

   (c) situational: contrast between what happens and what the character expects to happen

6. sarcasm: form of verbal irony; sneering taunt

7. hyperbole: exaggerated statement used for effect

8. rhetorical question: question asked only for effect, not to get information; has an obvious answer

# Initiating Activities

1. Place the play's title on an overhead transparency. Have students brainstorm what they think the title indicates. Have them study the drawing on the front cover, read the synopsis on the back cover, and make predictions about the plot.

2. Conduct a pre-arranged demonstration in which someone rushes through the classroom acting and speaking erratically. Have students write down their observations as eyewitnesses to the incident. Have a class discussion about what students think they observed and what really happened.

3. Place the phrase from the Pledge of Allegiance, "with liberty and justice for all," on an overhead transparency. Have students freewrite for five minutes about "liberty" and "justice" in the U.S. legal system.

4. Present the legal and literary terms from "Background Information" to the class (see pp. 4–5 of this guide). Have students list ten legal or literary terms and tell how they think these will be important to the play.

5. Create a three-column class chart on which you list characteristics of a novel in the first column, characteristics of a play in the second, and common characteristics of the two genres in the third column.

6. Play 10–15 minutes of the 1957 movie version of the play (available on DVD). Have students write a short response to the film clip.

# Suggested Teaching Strategy

A playwright intends for a play to be acted onstage, not read silently. Students will gain a deeper appreciation for *Twelve Angry Men* if they read it aloud. By assigning sections a day in advance, students have a chance to go over their lines and will feel more comfortable reading the play aloud in class. Please note that profanity occurs several times throughout the play. Students can replace these words and phrases with other words if deemed necessary. Because the stage directions will enhance the students' understanding of the drama, have a student read aloud the directions. Reading and understanding the information in the Introduction by David Mamet will help the students understand the importance of the jury system and the literary elements of a drama.

# Introduction

American playwright David Mamet points out the importance of the diverse people who comprise an American jury and the need to set aside individual prejudices in order to reach a unanimous verdict. He contrasts "good" and "bad" drama and concludes that the unpredictable ending of *Twelve Angry Men* marks it as a good drama.

| Vocabulary |
| --- |
| ad-hoc |
| decry |
| Shul |
| jurisprudence |
| subsumed |
| maligning |
| hucksters |
| adjurations |
| idiosyncratic |
| mitigate |
| catalyst |
| egress |

## Discussion Questions

1. Mamet cites Eric Hoffer as the "greatest American Philosopher" (p. vii). How does Eric Hoffer believe America was built? *(He compares the building of America to the ability of volunteers under the WPA [Works Progress Administration] to build a road with little supervision but with diverse talents and desire to work. He points out that a group of intelligent workers built America by devising a plan and using their common sense and group spirit to execute that plan.)*

2. Analyze Mamet's explanation of the "two Americas," of "them" and "us," and how this relates to our system of jurisprudence. *(He believes there are two Americas, as reflected by the pronouns "them" and "us." The America of "them" refers to those of a different political persuasion than ours. We refer to the America in which we participate as "us." Although members of this group have different talents and interests, "we" join them in various activities and can usually find a way to unite with other members of our group on most issues. Mamet claims that this ultimate unison is the essence of America's system of jurisprudence.)*

3. Examine Mamet's discourse on the jury system. Note the metaphor, "we (the jurors) *are* the State" (p. viii). *(He emphasizes that the process of being able to unite is the essence of our system of laws, and the jury trial epitomizes this ability to unite for a specific purpose. Within the jury room, everyone is expected to put aside individual agendas and prejudices in order to reach a fair verdict. As convincing lawyers for both sides present their arguments, jurors must try to differentiate between truth and lies. They must decide if the defendant is a criminal or a victim and render a verdict that will determine that person's future. Jurors are instructed to apply the standard of "reasonable doubt," which may have different connotations for members of the jury, but they must assimilate all the information and reach a unanimous verdict. Because jurors are given this power, they are, for the period of time they serve on the jury, "the State.")*

4. Analyze the Biblical allusions to perjury. *(Mamet uses allusions from the book of Proverbs to reinforce his condemnation of perjury. According to these allusions, perjury can result from partiality. Jurors must weigh testimony carefully in order to detect outright lies, slanting of the truth, or mistakes in judgment.)*

5. Discuss Mamet's definition of "gang drama," and compare/contrast his view of bad vs. good drama. Examine his rationale for calling *Twelve Angry Men* a good drama. *(A "gang drama" places the protagonist in a situation from which he must find a way out. In a bad version of this type of drama, the audience can foresee a predictable ending, but a good version makes the ending unpredictable.* Twelve Angry Men *has no predictable ending and, for most of the play, the possibility for the jurors to reach an equitable, peaceful verdict seems impossible.)*

## Supplementary Activities

1. Research the development of the jury system in the United States, noting when women were first allowed on juries. Create a time line that details how the jury system has changed throughout history.

2. Name a play or movie you have seen that fits Mamet's definition of good drama, and explain why.

## Act I, pp. 5–17

After the judge issues his instructions to the jurors, the twelve men retire to the jury room to deliberate on whether or not a sixteen-year-old boy is guilty of killing his father. In the initial vote, only the 8th juror, who is unsure of the boy's guilt, casts a "not guilty" vote. Several of the other jurors present their rationales for voting guilty, including details about the boy's criminal background. Three jurors immediately establish their positions: #3—antagonism toward the defendant, #7—impatience with the proceedings, and #10—bigotry toward "slum" kids in general.

| Vocabulary |
| --- |
| lavatory |
| fluorescent |
| premeditated |
| mandatory |
| Exchange |
| monopoly |
| el |

### Discussion Questions

1. What is the setting of this drama, and what is its significance? *(The drama is set on a very hot summer afternoon in the jury room of a New York court of law in 1957. The bareness and drabness of the room echo the emptiness and dullness of the defendant's life and the struggle about to take place in this room as the twelve jurors decide his fate. The oppressive heat symbolizes the intensity of the jurors' task and the explosive, heated arguments that will transpire between them. The jurors' only "escape" from the tension-filled room will be brief visits to the connecting bathroom. They also cannot get the fan to work, which adds to their frustration.)*

2. What are the judge's instructions to the jury? What is the charge against the defendant? *(He instructs the jurors to try to separate facts from fancy as presented in the courtroom testimony and to deliberate honestly and thoughtfully. If they find cause for reasonable doubt, they must return a verdict of "not guilty." If they return a unanimous verdict of "guilty," the death sentence will be mandatory. The defendant, a sixteen-year-old boy, is charged with stabbing his father in a premeditated homicide.)*

3. Examine the significance of the jurors' initial actions and their conversation about the trial after entering the jury room. *(They seem ill-at-ease with each other, and it takes them several minutes to get started with their deliberation. Their activities include going to the bathroom, getting a drink, reading the newspaper, and opening the windows. Juror #8 stares out the window instead of interacting with the other jurors. Their conversations reveal that some of them were bored during the trial, and most have already formed an opinion about the defendant's guilt. Their reactions to the trial, to their roles as jurors, and to the defendant include nervousness, hesitance, impatience, sarcasm, prejudice, rationality, and arrogance.)*

4. Discuss the emerging roles of the individual jurors, and evaluate the effectiveness of the Foreman. *(Juror #7 establishes himself as the "jokester" and is primarily interested in a quick verdict so he can go to a baseball game. Juror #12 is impressed with the prosecuting attorney. Juror #10 immediately pronounces the defendant guilty of killing his father and reveals his bias against "those people" [p. 10]. Juror #3 thinks the case is open-and-shut and becomes*

*argumentative to prove his point. Rather than taking a positive stance, the Foreman is unsure of himself and wants to please the others. After Juror #10 jokes about taking a secret ballot, the Foreman has the jurors vote by raising their hands. He tries to defuse an angry confrontation when Juror #10 threatens #8.)*

5. What is the result of the preliminary vote, and what does this reveal about the jury? *(The vote is 11 for "guilty" and one for "not guilty." Seven or eight hands go up immediately and others more slowly. Juror #9 does not raise his hand to vote "guilty" until the Foreman is counting the hands. Juror #8 casts the only dissenting vote. Some of the jurors are absolutely sure about the defendant's guilt, but others are less sure. Juror #8 is unsure about the boy's innocence but wants to know the truth, revealing that he is a fair, just juror. Jurors #3, #10, and #7 reveal their intolerance as they challenge Juror #8 and demand an explanation for his "not guilty" vote.)*

6. What is Juror #8's rationale for voting "not guilty"? *(He votes "not guilty" because he doesn't know whether or not he believes the defendant's story. He does believe, however, that they should discuss the case before sending a boy off to die. He isn't trying to change the minds of the other jurors, but he feels the case merits at least an hour of discussion before finalizing a verdict. He becomes an advocate for justice for a boy who has been kicked around all his life.)*

7. Discuss the background of the young man who is on trial for killing his father. Do you think heredity or environment plays a stronger role in a child's development? *(The first sixteen years of his life have been traumatic. He has grown up in a slum, his mother died when he was nine, and he spent a year and a half in an orphanage while his father was in jail for forgery. He has lived with violence all his life, e.g., beatings from his father. The boy has a history of criminal behavior, including throwing a rock at his teacher, spending time in Reform School for stealing a car, being arrested for mugging, and trying to slash another teenager with a knife. Answers will vary.)*

8. How does the 10th juror stereotype the defendant and "his kind"? How does Juror #9 respond? *(Because he has "lived among 'em" [p. 13] all his life, Juror #10 believes all kids who live in slums are bad kids. He calls them "born liars" and believes the defendant is lucky to have gotten a fair trial because they "don't owe him a thing" [p. 13]. Juror #9 reveals the wisdom that comes with age when he asks Juror #10 if he thinks he has a monopoly on the truth and states that he must be an ignorant man who needs the others to point out certain things to him. Juror #10 obviously has a poor understanding of the justice system and is biased against certain groups of people. His anger towards #9 proves that he is intolerant of differing points of view.)*

9. Discuss the efforts of the other jurors to change the 8th juror's mind, and analyze how he negates their rationales. Note what this discussion reveals about the trial. *(Juror #2 just thinks the defendant is guilty because no one has proved otherwise. Juror #8 reminds #2 that the burden of proof is on the prosecution. Juror #3 alludes to the testimony of the old man who heard a fight in which the boy threatened to kill his father and who saw him running away. Juror #4 questions the boy's alibi because, although the boy said he was at the movies when his father was killed, he couldn't remember the names of the films he saw or the actors in them. Juror #10 brings up the testimony of the woman who lives across the street and who allegedly saw the boy stab his father. Juror #8 questions the plausibility of her ability to see through the windows of a passing train, as she claims she did. He accuses the 10th juror of not believing the boy but accepting the testimony of the woman, who is also one of "them," i.e., a resident of the slums. Juror #6 believes the boy's argument with his father is a strong motive. Juror #8 concedes that the people across the street testified they heard the father hit the boy twice and saw the boy walk away angrily, but he does not believe two slaps create a strong motive for murder. Juror #7 brings up the boy's criminal record and his adeptness with switch knives. Juror #8 attributes the boy's behavior to the beatings from his father and thinks these could be a motive for the boy's anger, but not for murder.)*

10. **Prediction:** Based on discussion, will any jurors change their votes to "not guilty"? If so, which jurors?

## Supplementary Activities

1. Create a chart that lists each juror by number, and write information about each as it is revealed in this section. Continue to fill in your chart throughout the play.

2. Make a chart listing the jurors' votes, noting the vote tally, the jurors who vote "guilty," and those who vote "not guilty." Continue this activity throughout your reading of the play.

3. Create an acrostic for the word "stereotype." Write a paragraph explaining your interpretation of the word.

4. Analyze the following metaphors—nose: horn (p. 8); bull: kid [Modjelewski] (p. 9).

# Act I, pp. 17–28

Juror #8 presents his arguments for "reasonable doubt." The jurors inspect the knife with which the man was killed; Juror #8 produces one exactly like it that he purchased the night before. After each juror has had a chance to express his opinion, the second vote changes to ten "guilty" and two "not guilty." Juror #3 becomes irate toward Juror #5, whom he presumes is the one who changed his vote, but Juror #9 reveals that his is the vote that changed.

| Vocabulary |
| --- |
| alleged |
| diverge |
| fable |
| milling |
| proposition |
| abstain |
| babble |

## Discussion Questions

1. What is the significance of the 3rd juror's revelations about his own son? *(In an unintended outburst, Juror #3 reveals that he is transferring his anger toward his own son to the defendant. When his only son was nine years old, he embarrassed his father by running away from a fight. Juror #3 then proceeded to "[make] a man outa him" [p. 18], thus creating an antagonistic father-son relationship. When Juror #3's son was sixteen [the age of the defendant], he hit his father in the face and left. Juror #3 reveals that he hasn't seen his "rotten" son in two years. Juror #3 obviously holds a bias toward other young men because of his son's actions.)*

2. Discuss the conflict between the Foreman and Juror #10 and the effect this has on the deliberation. *(The Foreman attempts to stick to the original plan of letting the other jurors try to convince Juror #8 to vote guilty. When Juror #10 accuses the Foreman of being a kid, the Foreman angrily suggests that #10 assume the Foreman's responsibilities. Although some of the other jurors assure the Foreman he is doing a good job, he becomes disheartened and tells them he doesn't care what they do.)*

3. What is Juror #8's response to the other jurors' attempts to change his mind? *(He admits the testimony makes the boy look guilty but tells the others that, although he has no positive proof of the boy's innocence, he has a peculiar feeling about the trial, and it has left him with unanswered questions. He doesn't believe the court-appointed defense lawyer did his job adequately, e.g., he let too many little things go. He suggests that the lawyer is possibly just stupid. He believes, if he had been the boy, he would have asked for another lawyer. He points out that, except for the two eyewitnesses, the evidence is primarily circumstantial. He questions the validity of the testimony of the eyewitnesses, whose statements were not adequately challenged by the defense lawyer, pointing out that people can make mistakes.)*

4. How does Juror #4 present a convincing case concerning the knife? *(He presents a sequential list of "facts" about the knife. He mentions the boy's admission that he bought the knife, cites the unusual design of the handle, refers to the storekeeper's identification of the knife, brings up the testimony of six friends to whom the boy showed the knife, and alludes to the boy's arrival home at 10 p.m. He acknowledges that the boy's story diverges from that of the State's at this point. Unlike the other jurors, #4 presents a viewpoint based on fact rather than personal prejudice.)*

5. Compare/contrast the defendant's and the prosecution's stories about the knife. What is the 8th juror's response? *(Defendant: He stayed home until 11:30 p.m. and then went to the movies, returning home at about 3:15 a.m., when he found his father dead. He claims that, during this time period, the knife fell through a hole in his pocket, and he never saw it again. Prosecution: The boy stayed home, had another fight with his father, and stabbed him to death ten minutes before midnight. He then fled from the house after wiping the knife clean of fingerprints. Juror #8 points out that it is possible the boy's story is true—that someone could have stabbed his father with a similar knife.)*

6. What tactics does Juror #8 use to support his assertion that someone else may have stabbed the victim? Analyze the response of the other jurors. *(After both Jurors #4 and #3 attest to the impossibility of another knife exactly like the boy's existing, #8 takes an exact replica of the knife from his pocket and sticks it into the table by the first one. Jurors are astounded and question where #8 got the knife. He tells them he walked through the boy's neighborhood the previous night and bought the knife at a pawn shop. Juror #3 calls the demonstration "a real bright trick" [p. 23] but denies that he has proved anything. Juror #11 thinks it would be an incredible coincidence for someone else to have stabbed the boy's father with the same kind of knife, and both #3 and #7 agree. In response to the 8th juror's remark that it is possible, Juror #4 replies it is not very probable. Juror #2 finds it interesting that the second knife is exactly like the boy's. Juror #3 refutes the boy's statement that he bought the knife to replace one he broke. Juror #7 sarcastically remarks that the defendant was going to give the knife to his friend but first wanted to use it for a minute. Juror #8 questions why the boy would have shown the knife to his friends if he intended to use it to kill his father. Several jurors believe the defendant lied, but Juror #5 is not sure. After heated discussion, #7 assures #8 that he will not change anyone's mind and that his stubbornness will only lead to a hung jury.)*

7. What proposition does Juror #8 make, and what is the result? *(He calls for another vote, this time by secret ballot, and offers to abstain. If there are still 11 "guilty" votes, he will vote guilty as well. However, if anyone votes "not guilty," the jury must continue its deliberation. The vote is 10–1 for a guilty verdict.)*

8. What is the immediate aftermath of the secret ballot? What does this reveal about the individual jurors? *(After hearing the one "not guilty" vote, Juror #8 relaxes and sits down. Juror #10 demands to know who voted "not guilty," and #3 accuses #5 of being the one. Juror #4 intervenes to stop a physical confrontation, and #2 mildly tells them to take it easy. Juror #11 stands up for the right to have an unpopular opinion, and #9 admits that he is the one who changed his vote. He states that he did so because #8 has been standing alone because he isn't sure the boy is guilty, and #9 respects #8's motives. Juror #7 interrupts #9 by going into the bathroom and slamming the door. The Foreman announces a break before deliberation continues.)*

## Supplementary Activities

1. Working in a small group, stage the testimony in court about the knife. Give each student one of the following roles: defendant, defendant's lawyer, prosecuting attorney, or the judge.

2. Explain your interpretation of the metaphor, "…this golden-voiced preacher" (pp. 26–27) in a paragraph.

3. As a class, brainstorm about the purpose of using verbal irony, such as calling the defendant "a very fine boy" (p. 17), a "fine, upright boy" (p. 21) and a "noble lad" (p. 24).

# Act I, pp. 28–40

Some of the jurors try to convince Juror #8 of the boy's guilt. As deliberation continues, information about the victim's violence emerges, jurors discuss the testimony of the two eyewitnesses, and tempers flare as tension mounts. Juror #9 casts doubt on the truth of the old man's eyewitness testimony, Juror #5 changes his vote to "not guilty," and Juror #8 presents his rationale for reasonable doubt.

| Vocabulary |
| --- |
| soft sell |
| marmalade |
| murderous |
| compulsive |
| primitive |
| bookmaker |
| insignificant |
| punchy |

## Discussion Questions

1. What is the difference between "no doubt" and "reasonable doubt" in relation to the case? (*"No doubt" is based on absolute, concrete evidence and/or a confession. "Reasonable doubt" refers to doubt about the testimony or the circumstantial evidence and is based on reasoning and logic. If the jurors have no doubt that the boy murdered his father, they will have a unanimous guilty verdict. However, if the jurors have reasonable doubt as to the boy's guilt, they will not convict him of the crime.*)

2. Examine the information about the background of the victim, and analyze whether or not this might affect the jurors' decision. (*The boy's father had been in prison and was known to be a compulsive gambler who consistently lost. He spent a lot of time in neighborhood bars, where he often got into fistfights. He was a tough, cruel man who never held a job for more than a few months. This information might suggest that the victim could have been murdered by someone with whom he served time in prison, a bookmaker, a man he'd beaten up, a woman he picked up, or any one of the people he was known to hang out with. Answers will vary.*)

3. Discuss the testimony of the two eyewitnesses to the murder and Juror #8's assessment of their testimonies. (*The old man who lives in an apartment right below the victim's testified that he heard the boy threaten to kill his father, heard the body fall, and then saw the boy run out of the apartment. Juror #8 questions how the old man could have heard the defendant that clearly, either through the ceiling or an open window. The woman across the street testified that she saw the boy stab his father through the windows of a moving elevated train, recalling many insignificant details. Juror #8 doesn't think this sounds logical since the woman couldn't have had a very clear view from her vantage point.*)

4. What is Juror #9's assessment of the old man's testimony? Note the response of Juror #10. *(After watching the old man closely during his testimony, Juror #9 observes that he is old, poor, and physically impaired. He concludes that he is a quiet, frightened man who feels insignificant, has never received any recognition in his 75 years, and now feels that he is nothing. Juror #9 implies that the old man's need to be recognized, listened to, and quoted leads him to misrepresent what he saw and heard the night of the murder. He finally has a chance to be heard, and he wants his "moment of glory." Juror #10 embarrasses #9 by saying he has made up the story.)*

5. Discuss the commonality of the phrase, "I'm going to kill you" (p. 37), and correlate this with the trial. Note the reaction of the jurors. *(Juror #8 points out that each of the jurors has used the phrase "kill you" repeatedly to express displeasure and/or anger, but this does not mean they intend to kill someone. The jurors' reactions include validation of #8's point [#2], anger that the testimony is being questioned [#3], prejudice against the defendant [#10], changing a vote [#5], and disbelief mixed with sarcasm [#7].)*

6. What is Juror #8's opinion of the defendant's lawyer? *(He believes that the court-appointed lawyer obviously did not believe in the boy's innocence and insufficiently defended him. He asserts that the young lawyer might have resented being appointed to a case that brought him nothing, e.g., money, glory, a chance of winning.)*

7. What question does Juror #11 raise during the deliberations concerning the defendant's return to the scene of the crime? What are the responses of the other jurors? *(Juror #11 wonders why, if he is guilty, the boy returned home three hours after the murder, knowing he might be caught. Juror #3 sarcastically replies that he came home to get his knife because "it's not nice to leave knives sticking around in people's chests" [p. 39]. Juror #4 believes the boy panicked and ran away but later realized that he had to get the knife before the police did. Juror #11 challenges #3, saying the boy would not have come home three hours after the murder because he would be afraid police would be there. Juror #11 also counters the 12th juror's opinion that the boy would have gone back for the knife, thinking no one had yet discovered the body, by alluding to the woman's testimony that she screamed and called the police a moment after witnessing the murder.)*

8. Analyze the irony on page 37. *(Juror #10, referring to #11, uses incorrect grammar when he says, "He don't even speak good English" [p. 37]. The reader recognizes that #11 is by far more educated and speaks better English than #10, even though English is not #11's first language.)*

## Supplementary Activities

1. Write a poem expressing the 8th juror's thoughts as he stands alone following Juror #6's question, "Suppose you talk us all outa this and the kid really did knife his father?" (p. 30).

2. Identify the two things being compared in the simile, "[Talking to Juror #8 is] like talking into a dead phone" (p. 32), and explain your interpretation in a brief essay.

## Act I, pp. 40–48

Juror #8 calls for another vote, and Juror #11 changes his vote to "not guilty," making the vote 8–4 in favor of "guilty." Juror #8 presents a reenactment that casts doubt on the plausibility of the old man's testimony that he saw the boy running from the victim's apartment. Jurors #3, #7, and #10 remain argumentative throughout the deliberations. Act I ends with Juror #3 threatening to kill Juror #8.

| Vocabulary |
| --- |
| punk |
| railroad flat |
| hairsplitters |
| charades |
| sanctimonious |
| public avenger |
| sadist |

### Discussion Questions

1.  What is the result of the vote following the discussion about the defendant's returning home after the murder? What are the responses of the jurors who vote "guilty"? *(This vote reveals a change in the dynamics of the deliberations as Juror #11 joins #8, #9, and #5 in voting "not guilty." Juror #3 believes they are all going crazy. He enlists the aid of Juror #4 to present the "facts" and demands to know why #11 changed his vote. Juror #3 accuses those who voted "not guilty" of feeling sorry for the defendant and challenges the 11th juror's right to have reasonable doubt. Juror #7 believes they should accept the validity of the old man's testimony. The jurors who voted "guilty" are frustrated with those who voted "not guilty.")*

2.  Why does Juror #8 request to see a diagram of the apartment? Why are the points that #8 raises about the layout of the apartment important? *(Juror #7 refers to the old man's "running" to the door, and this sets Juror #8 to wondering how an old, crippled man could get from his bed to his front door in 15 seconds. After staging a reenactment of the old man's story, Juror #8 proves that it takes at least 42 seconds to get from the bed to the front door. This point is important because it proves the implausibility of the old man's story and his unreliability as an eyewitness.)*

3.  Analyze the significance and irony of Juror #3's comment about the old man, "Half the time he was confused. How could he be positive about anything?" (p. 43). *(Juror #3 is contradicting his own statement that reasonable doubt is nothing but words. In trying to reinforce his belief in the old man's testimony, he refers to the witness's confusion and questions his ability to be positive about anything, thereby negating his own point about the old man's reliability.)*

4.  What are the reactions of the jurors to the reenactment of the old man's eyewitness account of the murder? Analyze what the responses of Jurors #3 and #10 reveal about them. *(Juror #3 thinks it is a waste of time, and it will be impossible to recreate the scene. Juror #10 wavers between two opinions: [1] the boy's lawyer would have brought it up if it had been important and, [2] when confronted about the validity of this opinion, #10 states the lawyer didn't bring it up because it would have hurt his case. Juror #12 questions what the reenactment proves, and #7 sarcastically jokes about #8. Juror #9 points out that the walk would be long for someone who has had a stroke, and #11 concurs with him. Jurors #12, #6, #9, #5, and #2 believe the demonstration is valuable.)*

5.  Discuss Juror #7's use of sarcasm on pages 42 and 44. Why does he speak this way? *(Juror #7 makes fun of Juror #8 for asking to see a diagram of the apartment by asking, "Why don't we have them run the trial over just so you can get everything straight?" [p. 42]. He further mocks #8 by suggesting that he "ought to be down in Atlantic City at that hairsplitters' convention" [p. 44]. In both instances, as is true throughout the play, #7 uses sarcasm to draw attention to himself and to intimidate others.)*

6. Analyze the confrontation between Jurors #8 and #3. *(After #8's demonstration of the implausibility of the old man's testimony, Juror #3 goes into an angry tirade, calls the demonstration dishonest, and accuses Juror #8 of playing on the sympathies of the other jurors. When Juror #3 pronounces the boy guilty and vows "he's got to burn" [p. 47], #8 asks if #3 is the boy's executioner. Juror #3 assures him that he would like to "pull the switch" [p. 47]. Juror #8 accuses #3 of behaving like a self-appointed public avenger who wants to see the boy die because of his personal wish, not because of the facts. Violently angry, Juror #3 lunges for #8 and, when restrained, vows that he will kill him. Reflecting back on their earlier discussion about the phrase, "I'm going to kill you" [p. 37], #8 calmly replies that he doesn't think #3 really means he'll kill him.)*

7. **Prediction:** What will result from the confrontation between Jurors #8 and #3 at the close of Act I?

## Supplementary Activities

1. Draw a blueprint of the apartment, and trace the old man's path according to his eyewitness testimony. Write a paragraph explaining whether you think his story is plausible.

2. Working in a small group, reenact Juror #8's demonstration intended to disprove the old man's testimony.

3. Write a short explanation of how you would vote at this point in the jury's deliberation. Be sure to include whether your vote has changed in light of recent developments. If your vote has changed, explain why.

## Act II, pp. 49–63

The situation remains tense as the curtain rises on Act II. Juror #11, a European immigrant, emerges as a strong spokesman for justice. The fourth vote is 6–6. The debate continues, but a rainstorm momentarily distracts the jurors. Some of the jurors believe they should declare themselves a "hung jury," but others override them. They discuss the plausibility of the defendant's alibi and the distinctive pattern of the knife thrust. One by one, the jurors begin to change their votes to "not guilty."

| Vocabulary |
| --- |
| perceptibly |
| oppressively |
| bulldozed |
| even-steven |
| logic |
| infallible |
| inkblots |
| paranoid |
| gingerly |

### Discussion Questions

1. What is the significance of the opening scene of Act II? Analyze the symbolism of the weather. *(The jurors are in the same positions as at the end of Act I, and all are looking at Juror #3. During the awkward silence, he crosses to the window and defensively asks what they are staring at. Juror #12 suggests they start deliberating again, and #2 expresses the hope that they can finish and get home that night. Juror #6 suggests that they take another vote. The weather is oppressively hot, and the gathering storm creates an early darkness. Juror #4, who has remained reasonably calm, seems unaffected by the heat. Symbolically, the jurors have become increasingly heated in their deliberations and now face a verbal "storm" as they try to reach a verdict. Rain begins to pour down, creating the only sound in the room. Just as the rain lowers the temperature outside, the jurors must allow their emotions to cool down if they hope to reach a unanimous verdict.)*

2. What is the significance of the 11th juror's discourse on democracy? Do you agree with his statements? *(He reminds the other jurors that they are not on the jury to fight but to fulfill their responsibility, which he believes is a remarkable thing about democracy. He reflects on the process by which they were placed on the jury and the importance of their role of deciding the guilt or innocence of a man they do not know. He reminds the jurors that they have nothing to gain or lose by the verdict and, therefore, they should not take it personally. Answers will vary.)*

3. What is the result of the first vote in Act II? How do the jurors react to the outcome? *(The vote is even at 6–6. Juror #10 retaliates by telling the jurors who voted "not guilty" that they are out of their minds for wanting to acquit "a kid like that" [p. 51]. In response to a reminder by the 9th juror that facts, not the character of the defendant, should determine the case, #3 retorts that he is sick and tired of facts. Jurors #7 and #10 continue to argue for conviction, but #2 begins to assert his own opinion about the trial's omission of details. Juror #3 claims he was "baited" into growing angry by the other jurors.)*

4. Discuss the interaction between Jurors #3, #10, and #4 in the washroom following the vote. *(Juror #10 thinks the 6–6 vote is a joke but doesn't think those who voted "guilty" have a chance of changing the others' minds. Juror #4 believes they can do so by using logic, but #10 is ready to quit and thinks they should declare themselves a hung jury. Juror #3 disagrees and believes it is dishonest to quit.)*

5. Assess the role Juror #11 plays in the jury deliberations. Analyze the response of other jurors. *(Juror #11 is a voice of reason—logical, fair, just—and has an appreciation for the law. His attempt to clarify the meaning of "reasonable doubt" arouses anger from #7, who reveals his prejudice against immigrants. Juror #5 defends #11, who just wants to keep peace among the jurors. The Foreman asserts some authority at this point and tries to get the jurors to refocus on the trial.)*

6. What points do Jurors #8 and #4 make concerning the defendant's alibi that he was at the movies when the murder occurred? Note Juror #4's physical actions. *(Juror #8 brings up the point #4 has made about the invalidity of the boy's alibi because he couldn't recall specific details about the movies when he was first questioned. Juror #4 is convinced this proves the boy wasn't at the movies that night. Juror #8 blames the boy's inability to remember details on the emotional stress the boy would have experienced during the interrogation in the apartment where his father lay dead. In response to the 4th juror's assertion that he could remember details under such circumstances, #8 quizzes #4 about movies he has recently seen. Juror #4 remembers some of the details but cannot recall all of them. He reveals the stress he feels by mopping his sweaty forehead with a handkerchief. Juror #9 believes this incident makes the point that it is plausible that the boy could have forgotten details about the movies he saw.)*

7. What is the 10th juror's reaction when the Foreman brings up the psychiatrist's testimony, and how do his own words trip him up? Analyze the 11th juror's response to the sarcasm of the 10th. *(The Foreman brings up the point that the jury has not yet discussed the psychiatrist's testimony about the boy's strong homicidal tendencies, and he implies that the boy always had murder on his mind. When the Foreman first refers to the psychiatrist's testimony, Juror #10 insists that psychology is phony and psychiatrists are crazy. When #11 stresses his point that just because the boy could potentially have murdered doesn't mean he did, however, #10 trips himself up by referring to the validity of the psychiatrist's testimony.)*

8. What information do Jurors #2 and #5 contribute concerning the thrust of the knife? How does this information create reasonable doubt about the boy's guilt? *(Juror #2 mentions the downward angle of the stab wound and questions whether or not the boy, who is 5'7", could have stabbed down into the chest of his 6'2" father. Juror #5, who is from the slums, has seen many fights in which switch knives were used and attests to the validity of the question Juror #2 raises about the angle of the stab wound. He points out that a switchblade has to be held differently in order to release the blade and demonstrates by flicking open the knife and slashing forward and upward. His demonstration raises reasonable doubt that the boy, who is experienced with switchblade knives, would have made an upward rather than a downward thrust.)*

9. Examine Juror #10's use of rhetorical questions, and analyze his intent. *(He asks, "Know what I mean?" repeatedly [pp. 13, 40, 51, 52, 58] to reinforce his own opinion and prejudice even when the other jurors obviously "know what he means." In referring to the psychiatrist's testimony, he asks, "If they said the kid is capable of killing, he could've killed, couldn't he?" [p.59], although the other jurors understand this possibility. He uses these phrases to make points based on emotion rather than fact.)*

## Supplementary Activities

1. Stage a question/answer session in which you quiz other students about recent movies they have seen. (Suggestions for questions: name of the movie, names of actors, setting, background music, etc.) Tally the results of memory retention, and report your findings to the class.

2. Create an acrostic for "democracy."

## Act II, pp. 63–73

Both Jurors #4 and #10 continue to attest to their belief in the defendant's guilt; however, Juror #4 bases his belief on logic, while #10 bases his on his own prejudices. Several jurors have reasonable doubt after deliberation concerning the woman's eyewitness testimony, and they vote 11–1 in favor of acquittal. As the play draws to a close, Juror #3 tries to explain the boy's guilt, but breaks down and joins the other 11, and the jury reaches a unanimous "not guilty" verdict.

### Vocabulary

gall
probabilities
safeguard
acquittal
immoral
ad lib
farsighted

### Discussion Questions

1. Analyze the hyperbole with which Juror #10 alludes to the defendant's "people." What response does this elicit from the other jurors? Note the ambiguity of "they." *(His anger and prejudice cause him to explode in a discourse in which he denigrates everyone with the same background as the defendant. His hyperbolic tirade includes the following: "they" are born to lie; don't know what the truth is; think and act different; don't need a big excuse to kill someone; get drunk on cheap liquor; are violent, vicious, and ignorant; put little value on human life or family; breed like animals; are multiplying five times as fast as "we" are; and are against and want to destroy "us" [pp. 63–65]. Juror #9 calls #10 a sick man, #6 tells him to shut up, #1 tells him to stop, and #4 [who has been his ally] tells him to sit down and not to open his mouth again. Juror #8 encourages the jurors to keep personal prejudice out of their deliberations.)*

2. What logic does Juror #4 use to convince the nine jurors who voted "not guilty" to convict the defendant? Assess the results of this discourse. *(He acknowledges that some of the points for acquittal are excellent, especially the one about the stab wound. He then judiciously presents the two points he finds most logical for conviction: the evidence given by the woman who actually saw the murder committed and the fact that she saw him plunge the knife into his father's chest "the wrong way" [p. 66]. He supports his opinion by pointing out how meticulous the woman's testimony was as far as the time line of when she went to bed and the trouble she had going to sleep. He points out the exact time, 12:10 a.m., when she looked out and saw the murder through the windows of the passing el train. She vowed that she got a good look at the boy as he was stabbing his father. Following this discourse, Juror #3 thinks #4 has offered conclusive proof of the defendant's guilt, #12 switches his vote back to "guilty," and #3 changes his mind in favor of a hung jury. Juror #4 proposes setting a time limit on the jury's continuing deliberations.)*

3. What observations does Juror #9 make about the woman who testified that she saw the defendant stab his father? Evaluate the impact of this observation on the other jurors. *(Juror #9 observes closely when Juror #4 removes his glasses and clasps his fingers over the marks they have left at the sides of his nose. This gesture reminds #9 that the woman who testified she saw the boy kill his father had those same deep marks on the sides of her nose. He continues with a description of the woman, who tried to appear younger than her actual age and who, though she did not wear glasses in court, had marks on her nose that strongly suggested she usually wears glasses. Other jurors concur with this observation, but #3 doesn't see the connection. Juror #4 acknowledges the significance of the glasses when #8 asks him if he wears his glasses to bed. Because the woman would not have had time to put glasses on before seeing the murder take place, #8 concludes that she thought she saw the boy kill his father but actually saw only a blur. This point convinces #12 and #4 that there is enough reasonable doubt to find a verdict of "not guilty." Although #10 still believes the boy is guilty, he doesn't care anymore and finally votes "not guilty.")*

4. What is the 3rd juror's reaction when he loses his last two strong allies? *(He lashes out at Juror #10 and again trips himself up by referring to the knife and other evidence. Juror #2 reminds #3 of his opinion that they could throw out all other evidence except the woman's testimony. Juror #3 argues that he has the right to his own opinion and attempts to sway others by stressing that everything in the courtroom proceedings points to the boy's guilt. He calls the others a "lousy bunch of bleeding hearts" [p. 72] and tells them they are not going to intimidate him. He accuses the jurors of twisting everything around. When the other jurors remain silent, #3 reminds them about the boy yelling that he will kill his father. When #3 says he knows "him" [the boy] and how "they" [other youths like the boy on trial] kill "you" every day, he is transferring his anger toward his own son onto the boy on trial. He feels the knife going into his own heart as if he is the victim and his own son the murderer.)*

5. Analyze the closing dialogue between Jurors #3, #4, and #8 and what this reveals about each of them. *(Juror #8 reminds #3 that the defendant is not his son but is somebody else, and #4 says "Let him live" [p. 72]. These two statements bring #3 back to reality, and he agrees to vote "not guilty." The jury finally has a unanimous verdict.)*

6. Analyze the closing stage directions. *(Everyone leaves the jury room except Jurors #3 and #8. After the 8th juror puts on his own jacket, he brings the 3rd juror's jacket to him and helps him put it on. Juror #3 exits, but #8 pauses at the door and looks back at the empty jury room, with the knife he brought still sticking into the table. The rain has stopped, symbolizing the cleansing of the air both outside and inside the jury room. The "storm" of deliberation is now over.)*

## Supplementary Activities

1. Write a paragraph that reflects whether you agree with the statement, "Prejudice obscures the truth." Explain why or why not.

2. Write a short explanation of your interpretation of the simile, "[Juror #12]…is bouncing backward and forward like a tennis ball" (p. 68).

3. Write a poem or a paragraph describing the defendant's reaction when he hears the "not guilty" verdict.

4. Using the Triple Venn Diagram on page 26 of this guide, compare/contrast Jurors #3, #8, and #10.

# Post-reading Discussion Questions

1. Using the Character Chart on page of 27 of this guide, discuss examples in the play when Jurors #3, #4, #8, and #10 experience the following emotions: (a) frustration (b) anger (c) anxiety (d) intimidation (e) humiliation (f) relief. *(Note: Responses follow the pattern of a–e. Juror #3—(a) amount of time spent on deliberations; (b) #8 calls him a sadist; (c) everyone else votes "not guilty"; (d) #8 reminds him defendant is not his son; (e) everyone remains silent when he refers to all the evidence; (f) end of trial; Juror #4—(a) failure of others to listen to his logic; (b) in response to tirade of #10; (c) #8 produces the knife; (d–e) unable to remember facts about movies he has recently seen; (f) concedes he has reasonable doubt; Juror #8—(a) recognizes defense lawyer's inefficiency; (b) realizes #3 wants boy to die because of personal issues; (c) blade stops an inch from his chest when #3 pretends to stab him; (d–e) no evidence of intimidation or humiliation; (f) relieved when #9 votes "not guilty" on 2nd vote; Juror #10—(a) toward #4 for using logic; (b) explodes angrily throughout; (c) vote of 6–6; (d) realizes he has only one ally left; (e) traps himself with own reference to psychiatrists; (f) end of trial)*

2. What is the defendant's background? Has heredity or environment played the greater role in his development? Correlate the statement "Violence breeds violence" with the defendant's background. *(The defendant has been kicked around all sixteen years of his life, lives in a slum, lost his mother when he was nine, spent a year and a half in an orphanage while his father was in jail, and has been beaten regularly since he was five years old. His criminal record includes throwing a rock at his teacher at age ten, stealing a car at age 14, and other miscellaneous crimes such as mugging and trying to slash another teenager with a knife. The boy's father had been in prison, was a compulsive gambler, often got in fights after excessive drinking, and was not steadily employed. The boy has grown up with a poor role model and has developed the same tendency toward violence as his father; therefore, his environment has played the greater role in his development.)*

3. How are the themes of justice and prejudice developed throughout the play? *(Justice—Juror #8 is willing to stand alone in order to see that the jury renders a fair verdict, even though he acknowledges that the jurors may never know the real truth. Through #8's calm presentation of facts and refutation of evidence, other jurors gradually begin to see that justice requires letting go of personal biases and searching for the truth. Jurors #9 and #11 play key roles in seeing that justice prevails. Juror #4 wants justice and is willing to vote "not guilty" when he can see the logic of reasonable doubt. Even Juror #3 finally realizes that his anger toward his own son clouds his judgment. Although #10 votes "not guilty" only because he is tired of the whole thing, justice does triumph; Prejudice—Jurors #3 and #10 personify prejudice. As the play progresses, the statements and actions of #3 reveal that his prejudice stems from his sour relationship with his own son. #10 is prejudiced toward anyone who is from the slums. The theme of prejudice reaches its peak in his hyperbolic tirade about "these people" as he reveals the depth of his prejudice based on the "differences" he points out. He thinks the jurors have a chance to get rid of one of "them" by declaring the defendant guilty, regardless of the law.)*

4. Using the Conflict chart on page 28 of this guide, examine the types of conflict prevalent in the play: person vs. person, person vs. nature or society, person vs. self. *(Person vs. person— Juror #3 vs. Juror #8; conflict develops throughout the deliberations and reaches its climax when #3 threatens to kill #8 because #8 accuses him of wanting the defendant to die because of personal desire rather than listening to the evidence presented; resolved when #3 realizes his bias, votes "not guilty," and #8 helps him put on his coat at the end of the jury's deliberations. Person vs. society— defendant vs. society—defendant is blamed for his father's death based on circumstantial evidence and inaccurate eyewitness testimony; he is condemned, in part, because of his background; resolved when the jury reviews all the evidence and finds him "not guilty." Person vs. self—Juror #3 vs. himself; conflict develops when his son, after years of his father's pushing him to become a man, hits his father and leaves; #3 transfers his anger at his own son onto the defendant, causing #3 to believe in the defendant's guilt even when others experience reasonable doubt; resolved when #3 finally experiences reasonable doubt and votes "not guilty.")*

5. Using the Fishbone Map on page 29 of this guide, examine the evidence presented in the trial and the details that lead to the resulting "not guilty" verdict. *(Cause #1: old man's testimony about hearing the boy threaten to kill his father, hearing a fight, and seeing the boy run away; Detail: Juror #9 questions motive of witness; Juror #8 demonstrates the impossibility of the man getting to the door in time to see the boy run away. Cause #2: switchblade knife found in victim identical to one purchased by defendant; Detail: Juror #8 buys and brings to the jury room an exact replica of the knife. Cause #3: woman's eyewitness testimony that she saw the boy stab his father; Detail: Juror #9's reference to obvious signs that she wears glasses, which she would not have had on after an hour tossing and turning in bed, raises reasonable doubt. Cause #4: disbelief of defendant's alibi because he couldn't remember names or details of movies; Detail: Juror #4 is unable to remember specifics about movies he has recently seen.)*

6. Using the Story Map on page 30 of this guide, analyze the plot development of the play. *(Setting—jury room, 1957, very hot summer afternoon; Characters—defendant [although never seen onstage], twelve jurors; Problem—jurors must decide whether or not defendant is guilty of killing his father; Conflict—[1] interpersonal conflict between jurors, e.g., Juror #10 and Juror #3 against almost everyone, but primarily #8; #7's impatience to finish; jurors who believe the defendant is guilty vs. those who have reasonable doubt [2] conflict surrounding whether or not testimony of eyewitnesses is accurate [3] conflict about the switchblade knife, e.g., whether or not the exhibited knife belongs to the defendant, type of thrust that killed victim; Climax—woman's eyewitness testimony refuted; Turning Point Incident—Juror #4 acknowledges reasonable doubt; Resolution—Juror #3, now the only dissenting juror, sees the truth about himself and votes "not guilty"; jury reaches unanimous verdict; Juror #8 helps Juror #3.)*

7. What types of irony can be found throughout the play? Give one example of each. See "Background Information" on pages 4–5 of this guide for definitions. *(Dramatic irony: Juror #10 uses incorrect grammar when he attacks #11 by saying "He don't even speak good English" [p. 37]. Readers of the play realize that Juror #11 is far more educated than #10. Juror #10 contradicts himself about the validity of the psychiatrist's testimony, but the reader and other characters realize the contradiction. Verbal Irony: Juror #3 calls the defendant a "fine, upright boy" [p. 21] and a "noble lad" [p. 24], when he actually means the exact opposite. Juror #6 tells #8 the others are a "nice bunch of guys" [p. 29], when he really means they are a lousy bunch. Situational: Juror #9 recognizes the motivation behind the old man's testimony, i.e., he wants recognition and attention. The witness is not the concerned, honest citizen he tries to appear to be, and his testimony is not received in the manner he intended.)*

8. Discuss the characteristics of each juror and analyze whether he is initially "active" (quick to make decisions and tries to get others to agree), "inactive" (hesitant to take a stand or make a decision in the hope that the situation will resolve itself), "reactive" (allows the views and opinions of others to determine his decision), or "proactive" (considers the decision that must be made, studies the facts, makes a decision, and takes responsibility for the outcome). Assess whether or not the juror changes during the deliberations. *(#1: assistant head football coach; preoccupied with responsibilities as Foreman; accommodative; initially inactive but becomes more proactive; #2: nervous and timid; it is his first time serving on a jury; initially inactive but gains confidence and becomes proactive as evidence is examined; #3: owns messenger service: prejudiced, volatile, accusatory; doesn't want to listen to logic; active; #4: stockbroker; logical and intelligent; proactive; #5: nurse in Harlem hospital; from the slums; initially inactive but becomes more proactive; #6: housepainter; makes up mind immediately but is easily swayed; reactive; #7: salesman; avid sports fan; sarcastic and impatient; active; #8: architect; logical and consistent, calm, wants to know the truth; proactive; #9: elderly, observant, sensible, and concerned; initially inactive but becomes very proactive; #10: owns three garages; sarcastic and impatient; bigoted, paranoid, loud, and volatile; active; #11: immigrant watchmaker; sensitive to others; rational and sensible; initially inactive but becomes very proactive; #12: works in advertising; indecisive; impressed by prosecuting attorney; primarily reactive)*

9. Analyze the effectiveness of sarcasm, hyperbole, and rhetorical question in the jury's deliberations. Give examples from the play to support your response. *(The use of these literary devices draws the reader's attention to interpersonal conflict among the jurors and to the obvious bias of Juror #10. Jurors #3, #7, and #10 use sarcasm to reinforce their views. Juror #3 calls Juror #8 a "golden-voiced preacher" [pp. 26–27] when a second juror votes "not guilty." When other jurors begin to change their votes, #3 suggests they declare a "Love Your Underprivileged Brother Week" [p. 41] in honor of the defendant. Juror #7 uses sarcasm extensively to draw attention to himself and to push the other jurors to view the situation as he does. Examples include retaliating against Juror #2 for not responding to him by saying, "You're quite a ball fan, aren't you?" [p. 9]. When Juror #8 questions the speed with which the eyewitness says he reached the door, #7 tells him he "ought to be down...at that hairsplitters' convention" [p. 44]. Juror #10 lashes out sarcastically, "Boy-oh-boy! There's always one" [p. 11] when Juror #8 initially votes "not guilty." He uses the rhetorical question "Know what I mean?" repeatedly to reinforce his opinion [pp. 13, 40, 51, 52, 58]. Jurors #3 and #10 use hyperbole in describing people from the slums. Juror #10 says the kids are born liars, and Juror #3 states, "You can't do a damn thing with them" [p. 17]. The ultimate use of hyperbole is found in Juror #10's tirade against "these people.")*

10. Based on a quote by Edmund Burke, "It is not what a lawyer tells me I may do, but what humanity, reason, and justice tell me I ought to do" (*Second Speech on Conciliation with America*, March 22, 1775), characterize Jurors #8, #9, and #11, and discuss who is the real "hero" of the play. *(Juror #8 is the only one initially to vote "not guilty" because he is unsure about the guilt or innocence of the defendant. He wants to know the truth and will do whatever he must in order to present all the facts to the other jurors. From the first of the deliberations, he establishes himself as a man who is driven by what humanity, reason, and justice tell him he should do. Juror #9 is elderly and initially doesn't think he has much to offer in the discussion, but he is observant and sensible. He respects #8 enough to vote "not guilty" on the second ballot. This vote opens the door for #8 to question the reliability of the prosecution's case and establishes #9 as a key "hero" in the ensuing deliberations. It is #9 who brings attention to the possible invalidity of the old man's eyewitness testimony. Juror #11 is an immigrant from Europe who is proud to serve on the jury and tries to make the other jurors appreciate their responsibility. His rational, sensible response to the psychiatrist's testimony counteracts the volatility of Jurors #3 and #10. Each of these three jurors is a "hero" in his own way.)*

11. Discuss the various votes taken, and analyze the dynamics that change each vote. *(Vote #1: show of hands, some vote quickly, others hesitantly; Juror #8 is the only one to vote "not guilty"; Vote #2: secret ballot, 10–1, with #8 abstaining; Juror #9 changes his vote because of respect for #8's willingness to stand alone; Vote #3: #5 changes his vote to "not guilty"; discussion of old man's testimony causes doubt as to his motive and whether or not he could have heard the boy yell "I'm going to kill you."; Vote #4: show of hands, initially 9–3, with #5, #8, and #9 voting "not guilty," but the vote changes to 8–4 when #11 switches; follows discussion of defendant's lawyer and whether or not the boy would have returned to get his knife; Vote #5: spoken open ballot, 6–6, with #2, #6, #7, #8, #9, and #11 voting "not guilty"; this vote follows a demonstration of impossibility that the old man could get to his door in time to see the boy run away and #3's vow to kill #8; Vote #6: show of hands, 3–9, with #7, #12, and #1 changing to "not guilty"; this vote follows discussion of reasonable doubt in which #7 verbally attacks #11, the dialogue between #8 and #4 in which #4 cannot recall specific details of movies he has recently seen, and #5's demonstration about the way a switchblade is used; Vote #7: 4–8 when #12 changes his mind and votes "guilty" after #4 presents his discourse on the unshakable testimony of the woman who saw the boy stab his father; Vote #8: 1–11, with #4, and #12 changing their votes because they have reasonable doubt and #10 because he doesn't care; follows discussion about how the woman could not have seen the murder clearly enough to identify the defendant without her glasses; Juror #3 changes his vote to "not guilty" after #8 reminds him that the defendant is not his son and #4 urges him to let the boy live.)*

12. What is the symbolism of the title and the weather? *(The title symbolizes the biases and problems the twelve jurors bring with them into the jury room. Each must face his own prejudices and/or come to terms with the past if they are to reach a just verdict for the defendant. As various jurors do so, they emerge with a clearer view of themselves and the evidence surrounding the case and are able to reach a unanimous verdict. With the exception of Juror #10, who remains biased and angry, the jurors are no longer "angry men" by the play's end. The weather throughout the play is hot and humid, which symbolizes the heated discussions and the oppressiveness of the case itself. Act I ends with the explosive confrontation between Jurors #8 and #3. As the deliberations continue in Act II, the weather becomes increasingly oppressive. The jurors must turn on the lights to counteract the darkness brought on by an approaching storm and the ensuing intense rainstorm. The weather symbolizes the increasingly tense conditions in the jury room. The rain falls as the jurors decide the fate of the defendant but stops as they reach their unanimous verdict. The rain cleanses the air, and the "storm" has passed as the jurors finally agree.)*

# Post-reading Extension Activities

## Writing

1. Write a diamante poem contrasting "guilt" and "innocence" as they relate to the trial.

2. Pretend you are a news reporter, and write an article covering the trial and the verdict. Use at least ten vocabulary words in your article.

3. Write a two- to three-paragraph story about the life of the defendant during the six months after his acquittal.

## Drama/Music

1. Working in a small group, write and stage a TV interview with some of the jurors following the trial.

2. Working in a small group, write and stage a TV interview with the defendant after the trial.

3. Working in a small group, write and stage a courtroom scene in which the defendant is declared "not guilty." Add appropriate lighting and background music. Present your production to the class.

## Art

1. Create a collage depicting the symbolism of the weather in the play.

2. Create a diorama of the stage setting.

3. Sketch your impression of the defendant as he appears during the trial.

## Research

1. Research changes in the jury system since 1957, noting especially the emerging roles of women, when and why juries are sequestered, and the remuneration jurors receive. Write a one- to two-page report using your findings.

2. Research current information about the death penalty, e.g., states in which the death penalty is still in effect and states that have banned the death penalty. Report your findings to the class.

## Viewing

1. View one of the movie versions of *Twelve Angry Men* (either the 1957 black and white production or the 1997 TV movie), and give an oral report comparing and contrasting the movie with the written play.

# Assessment for *Twelve Angry Men*

Assessment is an ongoing process. The following ten items can be completed during study of the play. Once finished, the student and teacher will check the work. Points may be added to indicate the level of understanding.

Name _____ Date _____

| Student | Teacher | |
|---------|---------|---|
| _____ | _____ | 1. Write two questions you would ask the defendant about his relationship with his father and/or about the night of the murder. Exchange with a partner, and answer the questions as revealed in the play. |
| _____ | _____ | 2. In a small group, write ten review questions about the play, and exchange with a partner. |
| _____ | _____ | 3. Write a poem about one of the jurors, omitting his number. Exchange poems with a classmate, and try to guess the identity of the juror in the poem you receive. |
| _____ | _____ | 4. Keep a chart of the various votes, noting the result of each vote, the jurors who change their votes, and why they do so. |
| _____ | _____ | 5. Correct all quizzes taken over the play. |
| _____ | _____ | 6. Share your Post-reading Extension Activity with the class on an assigned day. |
| _____ | _____ | 7. Working in a small group, share any vocabulary, comprehension, or literary analysis activities you have completed during the study of this play. |
| _____ | _____ | 8. Choose a theme from the play, and explain to the class how it is developed (e.g., prejudice, justice, group dynamics, anger, the democratic process). |
| _____ | _____ | 9. Write a review of the play for your school newspaper. Use at least ten of the vocabulary words. |
| _____ | _____ | 10. Select one metaphor or simile from the play, write your interpretation, and present your analysis to the class. |

# Triple Venn Diagram

**Directions:** Use the Venn diagram below to compare and contrast Jurors #3, #8, and #10.

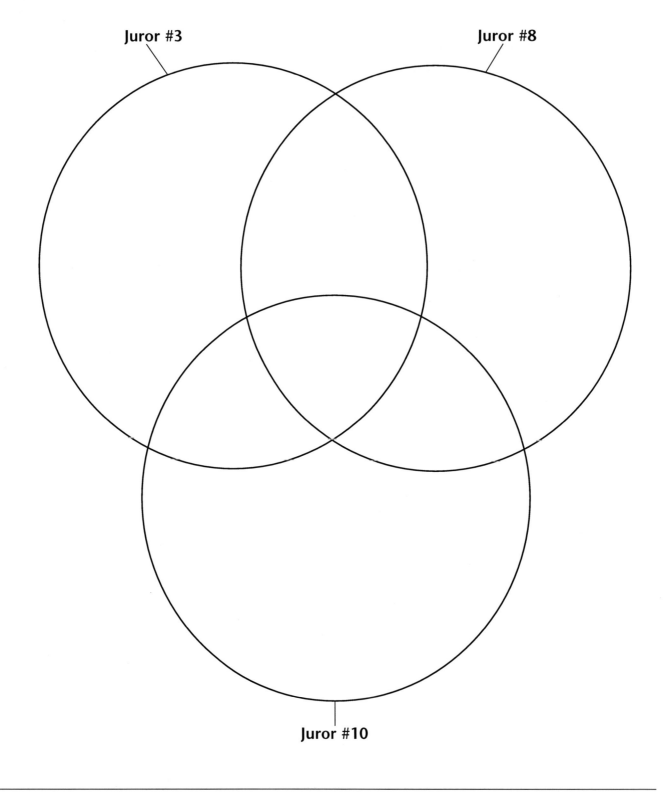

Juror #3

Juror #8

Juror #10

# Character Chart

**Directions:** In the boxes across from each of the feelings, describe an incident or time in the play when each of the listed jurors experienced that feeling. You may use "not applicable" if you cannot find an example.

|              | Juror #3 | Juror #4 | Juror #8 | Juror #10 |
|--------------|----------|----------|----------|-----------|
| **Frustration** |          |          |          |           |
| **Anger**    |          |          |          |           |
| **Anxiety**  |          |          |          |           |
| **Intimidation** |      |          |          |           |
| **Humiliation** |       |          |          |           |
| **Relief**   |          |          |          |           |

# Conflict

The **conflict** of a story is the struggle between two people or two forces. The following are three types of conflict: person vs. person, person vs. society, and person vs. self.

**Directions:** The characters experience some conflicts in the play. In the chart below, list one example of a conflict and resolution for each of the three types of conflict.

### person vs. person

| Conflict | Resolution |
|---|---|
| | |
| | |

### person vs. society

| Conflict | Resolution |
|---|---|
| | |
| | |

### person vs. self

| Conflict | Resolution |
|---|---|
| | |
| | |

# Fishbone Map

**Directions:** Consider the causes of the result in the box. List cause 1, 2, 3, 4 (as appropriate). Add details to support the causes you list.

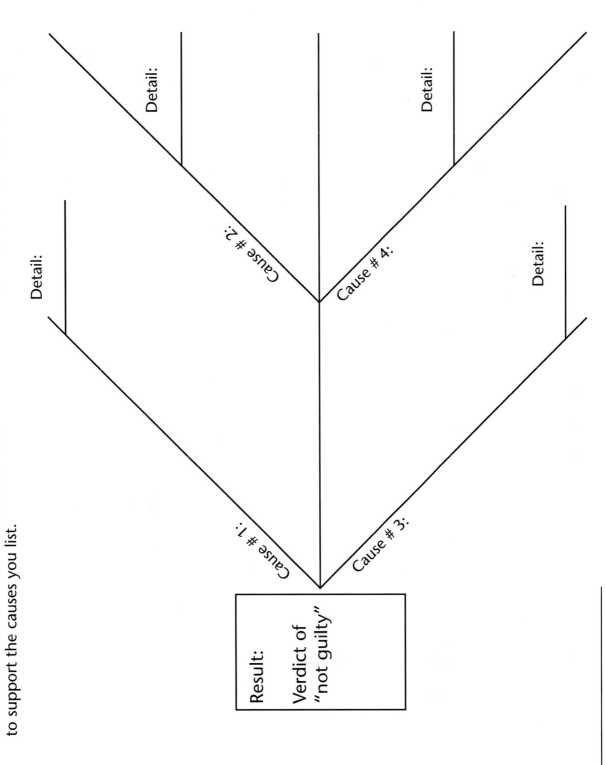

Detail:

Detail:

Detail:

Detail:

Cause # 2:

Cause # 4:

Cause # 1:

Cause # 3:

Result:
Verdict of "not guilty"

# Story Map

**Directions:** Fill in the story map below for *Twelve Angry Men*.

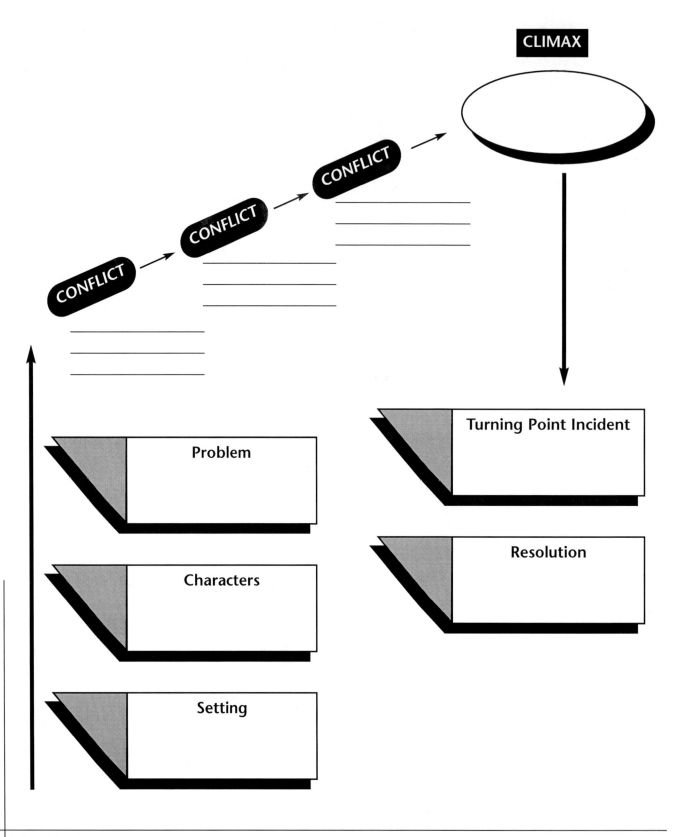

# Linking Novel Units® Lessons to National and State Reading Assessments

During the past several years, an increasing number of students have faced some form of state-mandated competency testing in reading. Many states now administer state-developed assessments to measure the skills and knowledge emphasized in their particular reading curriculum. The discussion questions and post-reading questions in this Novel Units® Teacher Guide make excellent open-ended comprehension questions and may be used throughout the daily lessons as practice activities. The rubric below provides important information for evaluating responses to open-ended comprehension questions. Teachers may also use scoring rubrics provided for their own state's competency test.

*Please note:* The Novel Units® Student Packet contains optional open-ended questions in a format similar to many national and state reading assessments.

## Scoring Rubric for Open-Ended Items

| | |
|---|---|
| **3-Exemplary** | Thorough, complete ideas/information<br>Clear organization throughout<br>Logical reasoning/conclusions<br>Thorough understanding of reading task<br>Accurate, complete response |
| **2-Sufficient** | Many relevant ideas/pieces of information<br>Clear organization throughout most of response<br>Minor problems in logical reasoning/conclusions<br>General understanding of reading task<br>Generally accurate and complete response |
| **1-Partially Sufficient** | Minimally relevant ideas/information<br>Obvious gaps in organization<br>Obvious problems in logical reasoning/conclusions<br>Minimal understanding of reading task<br>Inaccuracies/incomplete response |
| **0-Insufficient** | Irrelevant ideas/information<br>No coherent organization<br>Major problems in logical reasoning/conclusions<br>Little or no understanding of reading task<br>Generally inaccurate/incomplete response |

# Glossary

## Introduction

1. ad-hoc: for a specific purpose
2. decry: denounce; express strong disapproval of
3. Shul: synagogue
4. jurisprudence: system of laws
5. subsumed: taken into or included in a larger class
6. maligning: slandering; speaking evil of
7. hucksters: persons in the advertising business looking for big profits
8. adjurations: solemn appeals or commands
9. idiosyncratic: having to do with or caused by peculiarity of behavior or opinion
10. mitigate: make less harsh; alleviate
11. catalyst: person or thing that brings about change without being directly affected
12. egress: a way out; exit

## Act I, pp. 5–17

1. lavatory: bathroom; a room where people can wash their hands or faces
2. fluorescent: type of light produced by emission of electromagnetic radiation
3. premeditated: planned beforehand
4. mandatory: required by a command or order
5. Exchange: New York Stock Exchange; place where stocks are bought, sold, and/or traded
6. monopoly: exclusive control or right
7. el: elevated railroad

## Act I, pp. 17–28

1. alleged: asserted; supposed
2. diverge: move away from; deviate
3. fable: untrue story; fabrication
4. milling: moving about uncertainly
5. proposition: proposal; something offered for consideration
6. abstain: refrain; hold back voluntarily
7. babble: chatter; endless, often unintelligible talk

## Act I, pp. 28–40

1. soft sell: convincing by suggestion and persuasion rather than by pressure or belligerence
2. marmalade: jelly-like preserve containing pieces of fruit or fruit rind
3. murderous: extremely difficult or unpleasant
4. compulsive: caused or conditioned by an obsession
5. primitive: simple; original
6. bookmaker: a person who makes a business of accepting bets on contests at odds fixed by himself or herself
7. insignificant: unimportant, trifling, or petty
8. punchy: punch-drunk; dazed; disoriented

## Act I, pp. 40–48

1. punk: poor or bad in quality; miserable
2. railroad flat: apartment in which the rooms are lined up in a row like boxcars
3. hairsplitters: people who make minute, unnecessarily fine distinctions
4. charades: sham performance or behavior; acting out a word or phrase as others try to guess what it is
5. sanctimonious: making a show of piety
6. public avenger: person who punishes a wrongdoer on behalf of society
7. sadist: person who obtains pleasure from others' pain

## Act II, pp. 49–63

1. perceptibly: detectably; noticeably
2. oppressively: repressively; intensely
3. bulldozed: forced through quickly
4. even-steven: with the chances even; as likely to go one way as another
5. logic: common sense; reason
6. infallible: free from error; absolutely reliable
7. inkblots: designs made with ink used in psychological tests to determine characteristics of individuals
8. paranoid: condition in which a person imagines s/he is being persecuted or is very important; suspicious
9. gingerly: with extreme care or caution; warily

## Act II, pp. 63–73

1. gall: extreme boldness; impudence
2. probabilities: likelihood or chances of something
3. safeguard: something that serves as protection or defense
4. acquittal: the act of setting free by declaring not guilty; exoneration
5. immoral: morally wrong; corrupt
6. ad lib: make up on the spot; improvise
7. farsighted: able to see distant objects better than those at close range

# Notes

# Notes